Chestnut In Southern Maryland

Raphael Zon

In the interest of creating a more extensive selection of rare historical book reprints, we have chosen to reproduce this title even though it may possibly have occasional imperfections such as missing and blurred pages, missing text, poor pictures, markings, dark backgrounds and other reproduction issues beyond our control. Because this work is culturally important, we have made it available as a part of our commitment to protecting, preserving and promoting the world's literature. Thank you for your understanding.

U. S.—DEPARTMENT OF AGRICULTURE,—

BUREAU OF FORESTRY—BULLETIN No. 53.

GIFFORD PINCHOT, Forester.

CHESTNUT

IN

SOUTHERN MARYLAND.

BY

RAPHAEL ZON,

FOREST ASSISTANT, BUREAU OF FORESTRY.

WASHINGTON:
GOVERNMENT PRINTING OFFICE.
1904.

BUREAU OF FORESTRY.

GIFFORD PINCHOT, *Forester.*

FOREST MEASUREMENTS,
OVERTON W. PRICE, *in Charge.*

FOREST MANAGEMENT,
THOMAS H. SHERRARD, *in Charge.*

DENDROLOGY,
GEORGE B. SUDWORTH, *in Charge.*

FOREST EXTENSION,
WILLIAM L. HALL, *in Charge.*

FOREST PRODUCTS,
HERMANN VON SCHRENK, *in Charge.*

RECORDS,
JAMES B. ADAMS, *in Charge.*

LETTER OF TRANSMITTAL.

U. S. DEPARTMENT OF AGRICULTURE,
BUREAU OF FORESTRY,
Washington, D. C., June 28, 1904.

SIR: I have the honor to transmit herewith a report entitled "Chestnut in Southern Maryland," by Raphael Zon, a forest assistant in the Bureau of Forestry, and to recommend its publication as Bulletin No. 53 of the Bureau of Forestry.

The five plates which accompany the report are necessary for its proper illustration.

Very respectfully,   GIFFORD PINCHOT,
Forester.

Hon. JAMES WILSON,
Secretary of Agriculture.

CONTENTS.

	Page.
Introduction	7
The locality studied	8
The forest types	9
Silvicultural characteristics of chestnut	12
Occurrence	12
Soil requirements	13
Reproduction	13
Coppicing	14
Place of sprouting	15
Influence of height of stump	15
Influence of cutting season	15
Influence of age	17
Light requirements	18
Seed production and germination	18
Botanical and structural features	19
Growth in height	21
Growth in diameter	23
Taper	25
Volume and yield	27
Management of chestnut	29

ILLUSTRATIONS.

	Page.
PLATE I. Forest types of southern Maryland	Frontispiece.
II. Influences which affect sprouting vigor. Fig. 1.—Tree so weakened by rot that it has produced only one sprout. Fig. 2.—An old coppice chestnut; only a few sprouts produced	16
III. Fig. 1.—One-year-old chestnut from seed. Fig. 2.—Sprouts from stumps cut the previous fall	16
IV. Appearance of chestnut. Fig. 1.—Rough bark and characteristic root swelling typical of large chestnut from seed. Fig. 2.—Smooth bark of coppice chestnut	24
V. Grain of chestnut wood shown by the bark. Fig. 1.—Twisted furrows in bark of chestnut from seed. Fig. 2.—Straight furrows in bark of coppice chestnut	24

CHESTNUT IN SOUTHERN MARYLAND.

INTRODUCTION.

Chestnut holds a leading place among the merchantable trees of Maryland. Its cut is surpassed only by the aggregate of the several species of oak. It is used very largely for ties, trolley, telegraph, and telephone poles, rails, and fence posts. According to the Twelfth Census, the woodlots of Maryland (the wooded area of the State is mostly in small holdings) yield annually 4,867,000 board feet of chestnut lumber, valued at $57,682; 129,822 chestnut ties, worth $45,450; and 3,300 telephone poles, worth $4,300; besides rails, fence posts, and other material for home use.

Since it sprouts readily and grows rapidly, chestnut is especially suited for coppice management, which is one of the most profitable systems of forest management for small woodlots wherever climatic conditions and species available allow it. Consequently, this study of chestnut bears directly on the management of farmers' woodlots.

Though it is believed that some general facts concerning the management of chestnut as a coppice tree have been developed, the study is by no means complete, even for Maryland, having been confined to a small area within the wide range of commercial distribution of the species, and within the State of Maryland to portions of four counties, wherever cuttings for ties and telephone poles presented chances for getting data.

Limited as has been the study, it nevertheless establishes these facts about chestnut:

(1) Almost all the trees in southern Maryland are coppice.
(2) Almost all of these sprouted from the root collar.
(3) Low stumps produce the best sprouts.
(4) Winter is the best time for cutting.
(5) Chestnut from seed preserves the capacity of producing sprouts for a longer time than does coppice.
(6) Coppice must be cut earlier than trees from seed in order to produce good sprouts.
(7) There is an age when trees cease entirely to produce sprouts.

(8) Coppice grows faster than trees from seed for about twenty years.

(9) Coppice has thicker bark than trees from seed.

(10) Unnatural dimensions are called for by consumers of poles.

(11) Pure coppice is the silvicultural system to which chestnut is best suited.

THE LOCALITY STUDIED.

The study of chestnut in Maryland embraced portions of Anne Arundel, Calvert, Charles, and Prince George counties. Most of the data were obtained in the southeastern part of Prince George County and the northwestern part of Calvert County. They include analyses of 1,245 large chestnut trees and of 426 seedlings for the growth in height and diameter, of 338 trees for the taper, and of 1,690 for the relation between stumphigh and breasthigh diameters, together with measurements of 1,269 one-year-old chestnut sprouts for the purpose of determining the best time and way of cutting chestnut for coppice. The composition of the forest types in the locality was found by calipering all trees down to 2 inches in diameter breasthigh, on 16 acres of representative stands.

The area examined lies almost entirely within the Coastal Plain region of the State, and was once below sea level. The geologic formations of this area are, therefore, of sedimentary origin, and composed of unconsolidated clays, sands, and gravels easily eroded by water. As a result, the surface of the country is hilly and rolling, and trenched into deep, narrow valleys by the smaller streams. The hills vary in height from about 250 feet above tide in southern Prince George County to 30 feet in southern Calvert County. The climate is mild, with moderate winters and long growing seasons. On an average the annual precipitation is about 45 inches, with the rainfall distributed evenly throughout the year. Killing frosts rarely occur between April 20 and October 20.

The original stands of timber are mostly gone. The section studied was settled over two hundred years ago, and has remained principally an agricultural country ever since. Though the demand for chestnut timber in the early days was not great, it was extensively used even then for rails, fence posts, and vine props. The use of chestnut for the latter purpose is very ancient and widespread, since the distribution and climatic requirements of chestnut and vine are similar, and they are everywhere found together. In more recent times chestnut has been cut on a larger scale and at a more rapid rate, on account of the increasing demand for chestnut ties and poles.

THE FOREST TYPES.

The greater portion of the rolling land is under cultivation, but the steep slopes along the streams, which are not well adapted to agriculture, are left as woodlots (Pl. I). The wooded area may be divided into three general types according to the character of the growth and, to a certain extent, to the topography of the land. The tops of the higher hills and the gentle slopes are occupied principally by scrub pine, with frequently a small admixture of pitch pine and scattered specimens of red cedar. Several hardwoods capable of growing on poor soil, like black jack, post oak, and yellow oak, come up occasionally beneath the pines (Pl. II, fig. 1). Where the slopes are more abrupt and form ravines (or gullies, as they are called locally) the pines disappear, and hardwoods, with chestnut predominating, take their place. Though the hardwoods extend to the banks of the small streams at the bottom of the ravines, chestnut is seldom found lower than halfway down the short, steep slopes (Table I). Near the banks of the streams beech, yellow poplar (tuliptree), and sycamore become more numerous and attain their best development (Table II). Thus the home of chestnut is mainly the middle part of the slope, bordered by a pure stand of scrub pine above, and below by hardwoods, principally beech and yellow poplar (see frontispiece). Where the slope is gentle and the ravine broad the distinctions are not so marked; the types overlap, often giving rise to a mixed growth of chestnut and scrub pine (Table III).

CHESTNUT IN SOUTHERN MARYLAND.

The following tables give an idea of the composition of the different types, with the exception of Pine Ridge, which is covered with a practically pure stand of scrub pine:

TABLE I.—*Composition of middle slope.*

[Average of 7 acres.]

Diameter, breasthigh.	Number of trees per acre.															
	Chestnut.	White oak.	Beech.	Red oak.	Red maple.	Hickory.	Sweet gum.	Yellow poplar.	Black gum.	Scrub pine.	Persimmon.	Witch hazel.	Red cedar.	Black cherry.	Black walnut.	Other species.
Inches.																
2	2.86	1.14	3.71	0.71	3.71	3.71		0.86	0.86			0.29				0.14
3	3.00	1.14	3.14	.43	2.00	2.00	0.29	.57	.86			.29			0.14	
4	3.71	.57	1.57	.57	.86	1.14		.14	.14	0.14					.14	
5	5.86	2.29		1.57		1.29	1.43	.29	.29	.57						.14
6	6.43	2.14	.86	2.00	.57	.14	1.29	.29	.14	.14	0.29		0.14	0.14		.14
7	6.86	2.29	.43	1.14	.28	.29	.71	.14			.43			.14		
8	8.86	2.29	.14	.86	.43	.29	.71	.14		.57						
9	8.57	1.86	1.00	1.43	1.00		.57			.14			.14	.14		
10	9.00	.71	.43	1.00	.28	.14	.57									
11	6.86	1.00	.57	1.00	.14					.14			.14			
12	6.00	.71	.43	.71	.14				.14	.43						
13	6.57	.43	.43	.29	.29		.29									
14	5.86	.43	.14	.57			.14									
15	3.86	.29	.14	.29									.14			
16	3.43	.29		.43							.14					
17	3.29	.29														
18	2.00						.14									
19	1.71		.14													
20	.86	.14		.14		.14										
21	1.57		.14	.14												
22	.57															
23	.57		.29													
24	1.00															
25	.57															
26	.43	.14														
30	.43															
32	.14															
33	.14															
34	.14															
38				.14												
39	.14															
40	.14															
44	.14															
Total	101.57	18.15	13.56	13.42	9.70	9.14	6.00	2.57	2.43	2.13	.86	.58	.56	.42	.28	.42
Per cent	55.87	9.98	7.46	7.38	5.34	5.03	3.80	1.41	1.34	1.17	.47	.32	.31	.23	.15	.24

THE FOREST TYPES.

TABLE II.—*Composition of lower slope.*

[Average of 3 acres.]

Diameter breasthigh.	Number of trees per acre.														
	Beech.	Yellow poplar.	Hickory.	Chestnut.	Red oak.	Red maple.	Black gum.	White oak.	Mulberry.	Sweet gum.	Black walnut.	Scrub pine.	Sycamore.	White elm.	Other species.
Inches.															
2	20.74	6.67	5.93	2.96	1.85	2.96	0.37	2.22	0.37	0.37					
3	16.30	4.44	11.48	2.22	1.48	1.85	1.48	.74	1.85	.37				0.37	
4	10.37	7.41	4.81	2.22	1.85	.74	2.22	1.11	1.11	.37	0.37	0.37	0.37		
5	3.70	1.85	3.70		1.11	1.11	1.48	.37	1.48	.74	.37				0.74
6	2.96	3.33	4.07	.37	.74	.74	.37		.74	.37	.37				
7	1.11	1.11	1.48	1.48	.74	.74	.37	.37			.37			.37	
8	1.11	2.96	1.85	.74	.37	.37		.74			.37	.37			
9	.74	1.11	.37	.74									.74		
10	1.11	1.85		.74			.37				.37			.74	.37
11	.37	1.85		.37	.37			.37					.37		
12	1.48	1.11	.37	1.48	.74							.37			
13	.37	.74	.37	.37	.37	.37							.37	.37	
14		.74		1.11											
15	1.11			.74			.37					.37			
16	.37			1.48			.37								
17		.37		.74	.37										
18	.37			1.11			.37	.37							
20	.37			.37											
21				.74											
22		.37		.74											
23		.74		.37											
24	.37			.37	.37		.37								
25	.37			.74											
27					.37										
28		.37		.37											
31				.74											
33				.37											
34		.37													
36				.37											
40				.37											
42				.37											
Total	63.32	37.39	34.43	24.42	10.10	8.88	8.14	6.29	5.55	2.96	2.59	1.85	1.48	.74	1.11
Per cent	30.26	17.87	16.45	11.67	4.83	4.24	3.89	3.01	2.65	1.41	1.24	.88	.71	.35	.54

TABLE III.—*Composition of chestnut and pine type.*

[Average of 6 acres.]

Diameter breasthigh.	Number of trees per acre.						
	Chestnut.	Scrub pine.	White oak.	Red oak.	Hickory.	Sweet gum.	Other species.
Inches.							
2	3.00	0.17					
3	4.00						
4	4.17						
5	6.50	4.00	2.67	0.33	1.17		0.50
6	5.83	11.83	2.83	.17	.67		.33
7	6.83	10.67	.83	.33	.17		.67
8	5.33	10.50	1.17	1.00	.33	0.17	.67
9	7.50	10.67	.50	.67	.33		.32
10	4.50	10.00	1.17		.17		.33
11	4.00	6.33	1.17	.17	.17	.17	.50
12	5.17	3.67	.67				
13	5.50	2.33	.33	.50	.17		
14	2.67	1.17	.67				
15	3.50	1.00	.17	.17			
16	2.83	.33		.17			
17	2.67		.33				
18	3.17	.33	.83	.17			
19	1.67		.17				
20	1.83						
21	2.33			.17			
22	.83		.17				
23	1.17		.17				
24	.67						
25	1.38			.17			
26	.50						
27	.33						
28	.50						
29	.50						
30	.17						
31	.33						
32	.17						
33	.17						
34	.17						
Total	89.84	73.00	13.85	4.02	3.18	.34	3.33
Per cent	47.90	38.92	7.38	2.14	1.70	.18	1.78

SILVICULTURAL CHARACTERISTICS OF CHESTNUT.

OCCURRENCE.

Though capable of forming pure stands, chestnut hardly ever occurs entirely by itself. As already stated, and as shown by the tables, it grows in mixture with scrub pine on gentle slopes, and with white oak, red oak, yellow oak, red maple, pignut, etc., on steep slopes. Though found on all exposures, chestnut is taller and more cylindrical on easterly and southerly slopes. It avoids bottoms of ravines and valleys, as they are subject to frosts, to which chestnut is most sensitive; and for the same reason it avoids wet or cold soils. Hence it occurs more frequently with scrub pine, whose soil requirements are similar, than with beech, gums, or other hardwoods which prefer either heavy or wet soils.

SOIL REQUIREMENTS.

Chestnut is not very exacting in its demands upon the nutritive substances of the soil, but requires that it be deep, fresh, loose, and moderately fertile. The development of chestnut seems to depend more on the situation and the physical conditions of the soil than on its chemical composition. A moderate amount of clay, though not enough to interfere with the looseness of the soil, together with some potassium and lime, suits the species best. In Maryland chestnut is found mostly on fine, sandy loam, 9 to 20 inches deep, which is underlain by either a loamy sand or a reddish, sticky loam, which in turn may be underlain by a fine, gray sand at a varying depth of 3 to 6 feet from the surface. The soil is porous, well-drained, fairly fresh, and fertile. In mixture with scrub pine, chestnut occurs on coarser sandy soil containing about 10 per cent of fine gravel. This soil is loose and very unretentive of moisture; it is 8 to 10 inches deep, and is underlain by a coarse, sandy subsoil, which differs very little from the top soil. Chestnut also thrives well on soils derived from the disintegration of granite, gneiss, basalt, phonolite, porphyry, mica, or clay slates.

Chestnut is a deep-rooted species, which derives its nutrition from the lower layers of earth—a fact explaining its vigorous growth on exposures with poor surface soil. The taproot resembles that of oak in that at some distance from the ground it dissolves itself into lateral roots, which, together with lateral roots near the surface, form a widespread and powerful root system, the lower lateral roots often spreading through the ground at a depth as great as 3 to $3\frac{1}{2}$ feet.

On account of its deep root system, which makes it quite independent of the upper layers of soil, chestnut stands well and for a long time the destruction of leaf litter by fire or otherwise. Its dense foliage affords a good protection to the soil, and its abundant leaf litter, which decomposes slowly, greatly improves it.

REPRODUCTION.

Were it not for its sprouting capacity and its frequent occurrence on slopes difficult to till, chestnut in Maryland would now be a species of the past, as white oak and several other species are fast becoming. The conditions for the reproduction of chestnut from seed are very unfavorable. The presence of man, who has made a business of gathering and selling chestnuts, of hogs, which seek them greedily, and of coppice chestnut and other hardwoods, under whose dense shade the chestnut seedlings must come up, renders reproduction from seed almost impossible.

As can be seen from the following table, not less than 90 per cent of the chestnut in the locality studied is coppice, and it is undoubtedly due to its great sprouting capacity that chestnut still holds its own despite the hard treatment it receives:

TABLE IV.—*Mixture of trees from seed and coppice.*

Type.	Percentage of trees from seed.	Percentage of coppice.	Total per cent.
Middle slope	7.03	92.97	100
Lower slope	9.94	90.06	100
Chestnut and pine	11.32	88.68	100

The average diameter breasthigh of the trees from the nut is 16 inches, while that of the trees from the stump is 10 inches, which goes to show that a great number of young coppice trees and only a few young trees from seed enter into the composition of the woods.

COPPICING.

The capacity to produce sprouts from the stump (stool shoots) or from the root (root suckers) is possessed almost exclusively by hardwoods. It is based on a tree's capacity to form adventitious buds. These buds are entirely different in their origin from all other buds, and their occurrence in the plant world is less common than is supposed. While all other buds originate either at the tips of the branches or stems (terminal buds) or in the axils of leaves (lateral buds), and are connected with the pith, adventitious buds always start in the cambium between the wood and bark, and have no connection with the pith. They also differ from all other buds in having no protective scales of any description, the bark being their only cover. After a tree is injured, adventitious buds develop along the trunk or crown without regularity, or, if it is cut down, on the stump. They should not be confused with dormant buds, which are normal ones that originate in the axils of the leaves but fail to develop into shoots. The thread connecting the pith of the dormant bud with the pith of the branch or trunk elongates as the branch grows in diameter, in this way preserving the life of the dormant bud, often for many years, as in birch (ten to twelve years), beech (forty to fifty years), and oak and basswood (over one hundred years). Dormant buds that remain on the trunks or branches of trees for a long time lose all signs of having originated in leaf axils. Their connection with the pith of the stem or branch, however, will always reveal their true origin.

With the beginning of bark formation, and especially of fructification, the sprouting capacity diminishes considerably. Since the adventitious buds begin in the interior of the tree, and not on the surface, they must force their way through the bark. The thicker and older the bark, the longer it takes for the bud to develop into a shoot.

PLACE OF SPROUTING.

The sprouting capacity and place of sprouting differ in the different species. While some hardwoods, like most of the poplars, willows, buckeyes, elms, black locust, hornbeam, basswood, and beech, sprout most readily from the top of the stump, near the edge of the cut surface, others, like alders, ashes, maples, oaks, chestnut, birch, etc., sprout principally from the root collar. Of 1,245 chestnut stumps examined, 90 per cent sprouted from the root collar and only 10 per cent from the top of the stump. Under no circumstances was chestnut observed to produce sprouts from the roots (root suckers).

Sprouts from the top of the stump are less vigorous than those from the base, as shown by the following table for one-year-old sprouts:

TABLE V.—*Relation between place and vigor of sprouting.*

Place of sprouting.	Number of sprouts per stump.	Height of predominating sprout.
		Feet.
Top of stump	13.1	3.2
Root collar	25.6	5.1

INFLUENCE OF HEIGHT OF STUMP.

The height of the stump probably has some influence upon the place of sprouting, since the stumps that sprouted from their tops were, on an average, slightly higher than those that sprouted from the root collar only.

The following table shows the relation between the height of the stump and the height of the predominating shoot when one year old:

TABLE VI.—*Relation between height of stump and vigor of sprouts.*

Height of stump feet	1.0	1.5	2.0	2.5	3.0	3.5	4.0	4.5
Height of predominating shoot feet	5.3	4.7	4.3	4.0	3.9	3.8	3.7	3.6

Stumps 1 foot high show the best results, and, from the general tendency of the sprouts to decrease in height with increase in stump-height, one may infer that the lower the stump the more vigorous the sprouts.

INFLUENCE OF CUTTING SEASON.

The health of the stump and, consequently, the health and vigor of the sprouts can be impaired by excessive cold or heat. No season of the year affords sufficient guaranty against this, but the danger of the stump freezing or overheating is least when its water content is smallest, which points to winter or early spring as the best time for cutting. In the winter the water from outside sources, which settles between the bark and the wood, congeals, often separating the bark from the wood and weakening (in severe cases completely destroying) the sprouting capacity of the stump. To protect stumps from such injury it is advisable to cut them as low as possible, even level with the ground. Low stumps are easily covered with dirt, or in winter with snow, and so protected from the injurious effects of cold and heat, thereby preserving their sprouting capacity. Where low cutting of stumps is for some reason impossible, the top of the stump should slant enough to shed water. This precaution protects the stump from decay, which will affect the health of the sprouts. For the same reason care should be taken not to tear the bark from the wood of the stump when felling.

The following table shows the relation between the season of the year during which the mother tree is cut and the vigor of the sprouts during the first year:

TABLE VII.—*Relation between cutting season and vigor of sprouts.*

Season.	Height of sprouts.		Condition of sprouts.		
	Maximum.	Minimum.	Very thrifty.	Thrifty.	Not thrifty.
	Feet.	*Feet.*	*Per cent.*	*Per cent.*	*Per cent.*
Spring	7.4	2.6	11	53	36
Summer	4.4	1.7	7	37	56
Autumn	5.8	1.2		33	67
Winter	8.1	1.9	26	51	23

The table makes it evident that winter is the best time for cutting trees if good coppice reproduction is desired. It shows that trees cut in winter produced sprouts 8 feet high during the first year, and 26 per cent of all sprouts were very thrifty, 51 per cent thrifty, and only 23 per cent not thrifty; whereas trees cut in summer produced sprouts only 4.4 feet high, of which 56 per cent were not thrifty, 37 per cent thrifty, and only 7 per cent very thrifty.

Chestnut sprouts are exceedingly sensitive to frost, and when green and tender and not far above the ground, where frost settles most, they especially readily become victims of early frosts. The late start of sprouts from trees cut in summer leaves a vegetative season too short for them to grow tall and turn woody before the first frosts, which come at the end of October. Later in the fall, when grass is old and tough, the soft, green chestnut sprouts are tidbits eagerly sought, and, since they are near the ground, easily obtained, by cattle. The sprouts of stumps cut in winter or early in spring, when the sap activity is at rest ("the sap is down"), have a long vegetative season. By the end of October they are fairly woody, and above the lower frosty layers of air and out of reach of cattle. This explains why early sprouts are less frost nipped and browsed than sprouts that start late in summer.

Fig. 1.—Tree so Weakened by Rot that it has Produced Only One Sprout.

Fig. 2.—An Old Coppice Chestnut; Only a Few Sprouts Produced.

INFLUENCES WHICH AFFECT SPROUTING VIGOR.

Fig. 1.—One-year-old Chestnut from Seed.

Its occurrence far in the interior of a dense stand of scrub pine indicates that the nut must have been carried by means other than wind.

Fig. 2.—Sprouts from Stumps Cut the Previous Fall.

The leaves of the sprouts are still green, while the surrounding broadleaf trees are bare except for the withered oak leaves.

SILVICULTURAL CHARACTERISTICS.

Another advantage of winter cutting is that wood cut then is of better quality and greater durability. That is why many railroads specify winter as the only time for cutting chestnut and other species for ties. It is also to be borne in mind that stumps of trees cut in summer, when the movement of sap is greatest, often become weakened from "bleeding." This impairs the vigor of the root system, and consequently of the sprouts.

Since sprouts are exceedingly brittle during the first year, timber cut in winter should be taken from the woods before sprouting begins in the spring; otherwise damage may be done.

INFLUENCE OF AGE.

Chestnut is a long-lived tree, attaining an age of 400 to 600 years. It seldom remains sound, however, to an old age. Trees over 100 years old begin to grow hollow in the center, though their growth in diameter may continue for a long time.

The vigor of the sprouts depends upon the vigor of the mother tree (Pl. II, fig. 1) and the efficiency of its root system. This again depends to a certain extent on the age of the tree. In a general way it may be said that the most vigorous sprouts are produced at the period of maximum growth in height, which in coppice trees occurs in the first decade (Pl. II, fig. 2). In chestnut from seed the maximum rate of height growth sets in late (from the thirtieth to the fortieth year); hence seedling trees may be left uncut for a longer time without impairing their vigorous production of sprouts.

The capacity to produce sprouts is retained to a very old age, and up to a certain time the number of sprouts per stump increases with the diameter of the stump.

TABLE VIII.—*Relation between stump diameter and sprouting capacity.*

	9	10	11	12	13	14	15	16	17	18
Diameter of stump............inches..	9	10	11	12	13	14	15	16	17	18
Number of sprouts....................	13	18	22	24	25	26	26	26	25	24

The limit in sprouting activity is reached by coppice chestnut about the one hundred and twentieth year; in trees from the nut it is preserved to an older age. On poor soil and in situations exposed to cold winds the sprouting activity ceases earlier than on mild exposures and good fertile soil.

Large, vigorous stumps often produce 40 to 50 sprouts during the first year after cutting. Twenty to twenty-five years later, when the sprouts begin to attain merchantable size, there remain only 3 to 6 trees, the rest having been killed by the more successful competitors for nourishment and light. In order to save the waste of energy consumed in this struggle it would be of advantage to break or cut out many sprouts while they are tender and brittle, leaving only about 6 of the most promising shoots on each stump.

LIGHT REQUIREMENTS.

The demands of chestnut upon light are moderate, at least during its youth, as is shown by its dense foliage and its capacity to come up under pine. Nevertheless, light is one of the factors influencing the reproduction of chestnut from seed, as is suggested by the fact that on the mixed type of chestnut and pine, where the density is less than on the two other types in which chestnut occurs, there are more trees from the seed (see Table IV). Coppice chestnut is capable of enduring more shade than chestnut from the nut, contrary to European experience with coppice forests. Since sprouts start from stumps which have root systems already developed, they are abundantly supplied with nourishment, and are able, therefore, to dispense with light to a considerable degree. This is only a new demonstration of the long-known fact that light-needing species become more tolerant when grown in rich soil, just as the large supply of starch in potatoes enables them to sprout even in dark cellars. Abundant food in the soil compensates for lack of light, the function of which is to assist in the nourishment of plants. As a rule, the tolerant coppice chestnut has a dense foliage, and since several sprouts rise from one stump the ground is thoroughly shaded and the less tolerant seedling chestnuts are excluded. This accounts for the almost entire absence of chestnut seedlings on the middle portion of slopes, where 93 per cent of the chestnut is coppice.

SEED PRODUCTION AND GERMINATION.

Chestnut commences to bear seed when 8 to 10 years old and continues to do so to a very old age, but regular and plentiful crops begin only after the twentieth year. Every other year is a seed year, though chestnuts are borne in larger or smaller quantities every fall. Chestnuts on the edge of woods and in full enjoyment of light in the open bear seeds earlier and of better quality than those in the forest.

The yield per tree ranges between 1½ and 3 bushels, and even more in exceptional cases. European chestnut (*Castanea vesca*) yields 4½ to 6 bushels per tree, and occasionally 12, 15, and even 18 bushels. It should be remembered, however, that European chestnuts are much larger than ours, and fewer nuts are required for a bushel.

Fructification begins earlier in coppice chestnut than in chestnuts from the nut. Sprouts growing in the open have been known to bear seed when 6 years old. Coppice chestnut yields more seed than chestnut from the nut.

Chestnuts begin to drop in the fall with the first frosts, which are instrumental in opening the burs. The nuts germinate the following spring. Should the chestnuts be sown in the spring, the seedlings appear from four to six weeks afterwards. The capacity to germinate is preserved for about six months.

Chestnut seedlings are most frequently found at the tops of hills, among the pines, whose shade they endure fairly well. (Pl. III, fig. 1.) The nuts are brought there by crows and squirrels, and the habit of the latter of burying them in rows occasionally makes the seedlings come up as though planted artificially. Among the pines and on the edge of woods, where light conditions are favorable for it, chestnut produces abundant nuts, and therefore seeds the ground more thoroughly than chestnut grown in mixture with other hardwoods, which prevent its full enjoyment of light. This accounts, in part, for the greater reproduction from the nut in such places.

In addition, the thick leaf litter on slopes prevents the ready germination of seed, while among the pines, whose needles fall in the winter and cover the nuts, and on the edge of woods, where leaves do not accumulate deeply, the young seedlings readily succeed in establishing themselves. For the same reason, good reproduction from the nut is found on northern and western exposures, since the prevailing winds blow the leaves to the opposite southern and eastern slopes.

BOTANICAL AND STRUCTURAL FEATURES.

When grown in the forest, chestnut forms a slender, fairly cylindrical bole, and attains an average height of 100 to 105 feet. It grows taller and straighter on the lower parts of slopes than higher up.

TABLE IX.—*Influence of situation upon height of trees.*

Diameter breast-high.	Total height.	
	Bottom of slope.	Top of slope.
Inches.	Feet.	Feet.
10	69	64
11	72	67
12	75	69
13	78	71
14	80	73
15	82	75
16	84	77
17	86	78
18	88	79
19	90	80
20	91	81

In the open, chestnut assumes the habit of a fruit tree, developing a short, thick trunk and wide, spreading crown. As has already been said, trees from the nut grow more persistently and to a greater height than sprouts. They also taper less and have a thinner bark.

Within the locality studied, chestnut leaves are from 6 to 9 inches long and about one-fourth as wide. They taper to an acute point from a base which has a footstalk about half an inch long. They are smooth, dark yellow-green above, pale yellow-green below, and margined with sharp, upward-pointing teeth. The age of the tree makes no difference in the shape of the leaves; those of 1-year-old seedlings resemble in every respect those of grown-up trees. Late in the fall the contrast in coloration of the foliage of old trees and young sprouts is marked; the leaves of the large trees have turned bright yellow, while the young sprouts still preserve their green color (Pl. III, fig. 2). The leaves unfold late in the spring, and the flowers appear in June, after the leaves have grown to their full size. This appearance of the leaves and flowers after the time of late frosts has passed is an adaptation by which chestnut avoids the dangers to which it is so sensitive.

Male and female flowers are found on the same tree, and are borne on a central axis 5 to 10 inches long, which rises from the axils of the leaves. Male flowers preponderate. On the weak lower lateral shoots the aments consist exclusively of male flowers, and only the stronger upper vertical shoots bear aments of which the upper part is occupied by male and the lower part by female flowers. The female flowers are usually three in number, and are inclosed in a case that matures into a round, prickly, green bur, 2 inches or more in diameter. In October this bur usually contains three shiny brown chestnuts, the central one of which is the most perfectly developed.

The bark is smooth on young trees, but cracks and becomes rough with age. As a rule, sprouts have smoother bark than seedling trees of the same diameter (Pl. IV, figs. 1 and 2). The smoothness of the bark, therefore, may serve to indicate whether timber is from seedling or coppice chestnut. Rapidly growing specimens on good, fertile soil retain their smooth bark longer than trees having a slow growth on poor soils.

The wood is light yellow or yellowish-brown in color; the heartwood is readily distinguished from the sapwood by its darker shade. The sapwood very early turns into heartwood, and is composed of only three to four annual rings; its volume hardly ever amounts to one-fifth of the total volume of the tree. The annual rings are very distinct, the springwood containing numerous wide vessels, the summerwood less numerous narrow vessels, scattered in groups. When the rings are wide, the transition from springwood to summerwood is gradual, while in narrow rings the springwood passes into summerwood abruptly. The width of the springwood changes but little with the width of the annual ring, so that the narrowing or broadening of the annual ring is always at the expense of the summerwood. The narrow vessels of the summerwood make it richer in wood substance than the springwood, composed of wide vessels. Therefore rapid-growing specimens with wide rings have more wood substance than slow-growing trees with narrow rings. Since the more the wood substance the greater the weight, and the greater the weight the stronger the wood, chestnuts with wide rings must have stronger wood than chestnuts with narrow rings. This agrees with the accepted view that sprouts (which always have wide rings) yield better and stronger wood than seedling chestnuts, which grow more slowly in diameter.

The alternate porous and compact layers make chestnut wood flexible and elastic. It is not strong, but is very durable in contact with the soil, owing to the large amount of tannic acid which it contains. On account of the very thin sapwood, even small trees are of great durability; a reason why chestnut is of use when 10 to 12 years old, an age at which the majority of hardwoods have hardly any merchantable value.

Coppice chestnut furnishes better timber for working than chestnut from the nut; it is heavier, less spongy, and straighter grained, is easier to split, and stands exposure to the air longer; but its greater water content makes it crack at the ends after it is sawed. The wood of seedling chestnut is hard to split, and when split twists in all directions. The twisted growth of chestnut from seed may often be recognized from the appearance of the bark on trees standing in the woods, enabling it to be distinguished from coppice chestnut, the bark of which is traversed by straight longitudinal furrows (Pl. V, figs. 1 and 2). The wood of coppice chestnut is less "brash" than that of seedling chestnut; but it is more subject to windshake, especially on northerly exposures.

GROWTH IN HEIGHT.

Sprouts from a chestnut stump which has a well-developed root system put all their energy into height growth during the first few years. Often a height of 8 feet is reached the first year. Chestnut from seed must first develop a root system upon which to rely for its future life, and yearling seedlings seldom reach even the height of 1 foot. The life histories of coppice chestnut and seedling chestnut are therefore somewhat different. The sprouts grow rapidly at first, but exhaust themselves earlier than the seedlings, which start slowly, but grow more persistently.

Chestnut sprouts enter at once into the period of most rapid height growth, attaining their maximum average growth during the first decade. Later on, as the mother root system gradually becomes exhausted on account of the heavy draft made upon it by its sprouts (every stump, as a rule, has several sprouts), the growth in height rapidly decreases, and in the period between ninety and one hundred years is reduced to 0.1 of a foot per year. Seedling chestnuts grow slowly at first, while their root systems form. Seedling chestnut does not enter into its period of rapid growth in height until the time when coppice chestnut has almost attained its maximum height growth, and does not reach its maximum until it is 30 to 40 years old. After that the height growth commences gradually to decrease. When between 90 and 100 years old chestnut from seed still has an increment of 0.3 foot per year, as against the 0.1 foot per year of coppice chestnut. At the age of 120 years seedling chestnut equals sprout chestnut in height, and begins then to surpass it.

TABLE X.—*Rate of growth in height.*

Age.	Height.		Growth each 10 years.		Annual growth each 10 years.	
	Trees from seed.	Coppice.	Trees from seed.	Coppice.	Trees from seed.	Coppice.
Years.	Feet.	Feet.	Feet.	Feet.	Feet.	Feet.
10	7	23	7	23	0.7	2.3
20	17	42	10	19	1.0	1.9
30	33	57	16	15	1.6	1.5
40	52	69	19	12	1.9	1.2
50	64	77	12	8	1.2	.8
60	73	83	9	6	.9	.6
70	80	87	7	4	.7	.4
80	84	90	4	3	.4	.3
90	88	92	4	2	.4	.2
100	91	93	3	1	.3	.1
110	93	94	2	1	.2	.1
120	95	95	2	1	.2	.1

TABLE XI.—*Age of trees of different heights.*

Height.	Age.	
	Trees from seed.	Coppice.
Feet.	Years.	Years.
5	7	2
10	13	4
15	18	7
20	22	9
25	25	11
30	28	13
35	31	16
40	33	19
45	36	22
50	39	25
55	42	29
60	46	33
65	51	37
70	56	42
75	63	47
80	71	55
85	81	64
90	96	80

SILVICULTURAL CHARACTERISTICS.

TABLE XII.—*Height of trees of different diameters.*

Diameter breast-high.	Height.	
	Trees from seed.	Coppice.
Inches.	Feet.	Feet.
1	8	9
2	12	14
3	15	18
4	20	25
5	26	31
6	33	37
7	41	43
8	46	50
9	53	56
10	58	61
11	63	67
12	67	72
13	72	76
14	75	80
15	78	83
16	81	85
17	84	88
18	86	90
19	88	92
20	91	94

GROWTH IN DIAMETER.

The diameter growth of coppice chestnut and chestnut from seed shows a difference similar to that which has been observed in their height growth. Coppice chestnut commences its rapid growth in thickness early, soon reaches its maximum, and quickly begins to decrease. In chestnut from seed, rapid diameter growth sets in comparatively late, but it persists for a longer time. When between ninety and one hundred years of age, the diameter of chestnut from seed equals that of coppice chestnut, and from then on surpasses it.

TABLE XIII.—*Rate of growth in diameter.*

Age.	Diameter breast-high.		Growth each 10 years.		Annual growth each 10 years.	
	Trees from seed.	Coppice.	Trees from seed.	Coppice.	Trees from seed.	Coppice.
Years.	Feet.	Feet.	Feet.	Feet.	Feet.	Feet.
10	0.8	3.8	0.8	3.8	0.1	0.4
20	3.4	6.8	2.6	3.0	.3	.3
30	6.0	9.3	2.6	2.5	.3	.3
40	8.7	11.4	2.7	2.1	.3	.2
50	11.2	13.4	2.5	2.0	.3	.2
60	13.4	15.1	2.2	1.7	.2	.2
70	15.4	16.7	2.0	1.6	.2	.2
80	17.2	18.0	1.8	1.3	.2	.1
90	18.8	19.2	1.6	1.2	.2	.1
100	20.1	19.8	1.3	.6	.1	.1
110	21.0	20.4	.9	.6	.1	.1
120	21.6	20.8	.6	.4	.1	.1

TABLE XIV.—*Age of trees of different diameters.*

Diameter breast-high.	Age.		Time required to grow 1 inch.	
	Trees from seed.	Coppice.	Trees from seed.	Coppice.
Inches.	Years.	Years.	Years.	Years.
1	11	4	4	2
2	15	6	3	2
3	18	8	4	3
4	22	11	4	3
5	26	14	4	3
6	30	17	4	4
7	34	21	3	4
8	37	25	4	4
9	41	29	4	4
10	45	33	4	5
11	49	38	4	5
12	53	43	5	5
13	58	48	5	6
14	63	54	5	5
15	68	59	5	6
16	73	65	5	7
17	78	72	6	7
18	84	79	7	10
19	91	89	8	14
20	99	103	11	21

The tables show that in both chestnut from seed and coppice chestnut the growth in diameter continues at a good rate long after height growth has practically come to a standstill.

Its greater persistence in height growth and diameter growth enables seedling chestnut to attain greater heights and larger diameters than coppice chestnut, and to furnish, therefore, timber of large dimensions. But in Maryland the demand for chestnut lumber is not so great as that for ties, trolley, telegraph, and telephone poles, rails, fence posts, etc., and everything points to increased demand for the kinds of timber called for at present. Consequently the rapid growth of coppice chestnut at an early age, which enables it to attain the sizes demanded in a shorter time than chestnut from seed, gives a greater prospect of profit from raising coppice chestnut. Besides, chestnut over 100 years old is apt to become slightly decayed in the center. By that time it has also practically completed its height growth, and is tall enough to enjoy plenty of light. This prevents it from clearing itself further, and the result is a short clear bole in comparison with the total height of the tree.

Fig. 1.—Rough Bark and Characteristic Root Swelling Typical of Large Chestnut from Seed.

Fig. 2.—Smooth Bark of Coppice Chestnut. This is the Third Generation Despite the Bad Method of Cutting.

APPEARANCE OF CHESTNUT.

Bul. 53, Bureau of Forestry, U. S. Dept. of Agriculture. PLATE V.

Fig. 1.—Twisted Furrows in Bark of Chestnut from Seed.

Fig. 2.—Straight Furrows in Bark of Coppice Chestnut.

GRAIN OF CHESTNUT WOOD SHOWN BY THE BARK.

SILVICULTURAL CHARACTERISTICS.

TABLE XV.—*Clear length in relation to height.*

Diameter breast-high.	Height.		Clear length.	
	Trees from seed.	Coppice.	Trees from seed.	Coppice.
Inches.	Feet.	Feet.	Feet.	Feet.
10	58	61	28	28
11	63	67	30	31
12	67	72	31	33
13	72	76	32	34
14	75	80	33	35
15	78	83	34	36
16	81	85	34	36
17	84	88	34	36
18	86	90	35	36
19	88	92	35	37
20	91	94	35	37

TAPER.

The following table gives the diameter outside the bark at various heights from the ground, for forest-grown trees of different diameters breasthigh. If the diameter breasthigh of a standing tree in the woods is known, its height and its diameter every 10 feet above the ground can be found in the table. It will be seen that the tops, and in large trees the butts, taper faster than the middle portions of the tree. The difference in taper between trees from seed and coppice is not sufficient to warrant distinction.

TABLE XVI.—*Diameters outside bark at various heights.*

Diameter breast-high.	Height above ground—feet.									Total height.
	10	20	30	40	50	60	70	80	90	
Inches.	Inches.	Inches.	Inches.	Inches.	Inches.	Inches.	Inches.	Inches.	Inches.	Feet.
10	9.3	8.0	6.7	5.4	3.9	0.4				61
11	10.1	8.8	7.4	6.0	4.5	2.2				67
12	10.9	9.6	8.2	6.7	5.0	2.9	0.2			71
13	11.8	10.4	8.9	7.2	5.3	3.3	1.2			76
14	12.7	11.2	9.7	7.6	5.7	3.7	1.6			79
15	13.6	11.9	10.3	8.3	6.1	4.0	2.0	0.3		82
16	14.4	12.7	11.1	9.0	6.7	4.3	2.3	.7		85
17	15.3	13.5	11.8	9.8	7.1	4.6	2.6	1.0		87
18	16.2	14.2	12.5	10.4	7.6	4.9	2.9	1.3		89
19	16.9	15.0	13.4	11.3	8.4	5.4	3.3	1.7	0.2	91
20	17.8	15.8	14.2	12.0	8.8	5.6	3.6	1.9	.4	93

In many cases it is necessary to know the amount of bark to deduct in order to get the inside diameter, as, for instance, in cutting chestnut for telephone poles, which must be peeled and of specified dimensions. Therefore a table of the thickness of bark of trees of different diameters breasthigh is given below for both seedling and coppice chestnuts. It will be seen that the bark of sprouts is slightly thicker than that of seedlings.

TABLE XVII.—*Thickness of bark.*

Diameter breasthigh.	Diameter of bark.	
	Trees from seed.	Coppice.
Inches.	Inches.	Inches.
6	0.7	0.7
7	.7	.8
8	.7	.8
9	.8	.9
10	.9	.9
11	1.0	1.0
12	1.0	1.1
13	1.1	1.1
14	1.2	1.2
15	1.2	1.2
16	1.3	1.3
17	1.3	1.3
18	1.4	1.4
19	1.4	1.5
20	1.5	1.5

A table giving the diameter inside the bark at different heights above the ground can readily be made from the two preceding tables.

It is interesting to compare the natural taper of chestnut with that required by specifications from telephone companies purchasing poles in the section of Maryland examined.

TABLE XVIII.—*Comparison of natural and specified pole dimensions.*

Length of pole.	Diameter inside bark at top.		Diameter inside bark 6 feet from butt.	
	Natural.	Specified.	Natural.	Specified.
Feet.	Inches.	Inches.	Inches.	Inches.
25	8.1	8	10.7	10.5
30	8.2	8	11.6	11.1
35	8.1	8	12.6	12.1
35	8.7	8	13.5	12.1
40	8.3	8	14.5	12.7
40	9.0	8	15.4	12.7
45	8.5	8	16.3	13.7
45	9.0	8	17.3	13.7
50	8.4	8	18.2	15.0
50	8.8	8	19.3	15.0
50	9.4	8	20.2	15.0
55	8.1	8	21.1	16.2
55	8.6	8	21.9	16.2
55	9.0	8	22.9	16.2
55	9.3	8	24.0	16.2

SILVICULTURAL CHARACTERISTICS.

This table shows that poles with length and top diameter as specified by the telephone companies always have at 6 feet from the butt diameters larger than called for at that point by the specifications. Poles of given length, with butts as specified, have at their tops diameters smaller than is required. The telephone companies can, therefore, do away entirely with butt specifications, relying only upon top and length requirements. A pole of required length and diameter at top will always have a larger diameter at 6 feet from the ground than is called for by the specifications.

The specifications call for trees of slighter taper than the present woods of Maryland are capable of producing. In order to form the long, cylindrical bole necessary to yield such poles, chestnut must be grown in a dense stand, such as is found in virgin or artificially raised forests. On account of the greatly thinned condition of most Maryland woods, chestnut grows in a fairly open stand, and consequently produces a short, very tapering trunk and a large crown. The pole contractors complain that with the decrease in the original stands of chestnut and the thinning out of the few left it becomes harder and harder to find poles answering the specifications; that is, a tree with the required butt diameter is not likely to be sufficiently cylindrical or clear of branches for the required length.

VOLUME AND YIELD.

The taper of chestnut has been used to prepare a table giving the number of hewn ties which can be obtained from trees of different diameters breasthigh. Only No. 1 (8.5 feet by 7 by 7 inches) and No. 2 (8.5 feet by 6 inches face by 7 inches) ties were taken into account:

TABLE XIX.—*Number of ties per tree.*

Diameter breast-high.	Volume.	Length wasted.
Inches.	*Ties.*	*Feet.*
10	1	51
11	2	48
12	3	44
13	3	49
14	4	43
15	4	46
16	5	41
17	5	43
18	5	45
19	5	47
20	5	49

The waste of timber, which attends tie cutting, as shown in the table, is very great; but the demand for chestnut for other purposes is comparatively small, and ties will for a long time be the only readily marketable product. Hewn ties are preferred. Many railroads refuse sawn chestnut ties entirely, because their rough surfaces absorb moisture readily, and decay, therefore, proceeds faster than in hewn ties, whose comparatively smooth surfaces shed water. Trees 14 to 18 inches in diameter breasthigh are the best sizes from which to cut ties, as the waste is least in them. Trees above 20 inches ought to be sawed into ties, not hewn, since more ties can thus be obtained; and the larger the size of the tree above this point the greater the saving, for chestnut 20 inches and over has attained practically its maximum height, and since the clear length increases but little with increase in diameter, no more hewn ties can be obtained from a 25-inch tree than from a 20-inch tree.

The following table gives the length of telegraph or telephone poles that can be obtained from trees of different diameters. Not every tree will yield a pole, however. Besides being of certain sizes, the poles must be straight, well proportioned, and free from windshake or rotten knots. It is estimated that not more than 15 per cent of all trees fit for ties will make telegraph poles, and a still smaller per cent large telephone poles.

TABLE XX.—*Size of pole per tree.*

Diameter breast-high.	Length of pole.	Diameter at top.	Diameter 6 feet from butt.
Inches.	Feet.	Inches.	Inches.
11	25	8.1	10.7
12	30	8.2	11.6
13	35	8.1	12.6
14	35	8.7	13.5
15	40	8.3	14.5
16	40	9.0	15.4
17	45	8.5	16.3
18	45	9.0	17.3
19	50	8.4	18.2
20	50	8.8	19.3

From the knowledge of the number of ties in trees of different diameters and of the average number of trees of different diameters per acre, a table of the yield in hewn ties and their value per acre on the different forest types has been constructed. Ten cents is taken as the average stumpage price per tie. The application of this table must necessarily be very local, since it is based on comparatively few data representative of not widely differing conditions. It is intended merely to convey some idea as to the number of ties which can be obtained in the uncut woods of the region examined, samples of which were measured, and their results given in Tables I, II, and III.

TABLE XXI.—*Yield per acre.*

	Chestnut and pine.		Middle slope.		Lower slope.	
	Ties.	Value.	Ties.	Value.	Ties.	Value.
Trees 10 inches and over	180	$18	190	$19	60	$6
Trees 10 inches to 20 inches	140	14	160	16	30	3

MANAGEMENT OF CHESTNUT.

Consideration of the practicability of managing southern Maryland woodlots for the production of chestnut was not regarded as a part of this study. There was not time for going into the varied local economic and silvicultural questions involved in deciding when, where, and what to do. That something should be done goes without saying. What has been stated about the behavior of the species is enough to show that chestnut offers a chance for doing something worth while.

The silvicultural system to which chestnut is best suited is "pure coppice." It is not suited for "overwood over coppice," or for "coppice under overwood." In the former it would have an abundance of light, and form large, spreading crowns and short, tapering trunks, yielding inferior timber. As an underwood it would suffer too much from the dense shade cast by the overwood. Under "pure coppice" management chestnut would furnish a greater yield per acre of easily marketable products than if grown as "high forest." Chestnut from seed is more light-needing than chestnut coppice, especially in old age. When grown in pure woods as "high forest," it thins out early, and consequently has not so many trees per acre as do "pure coppice" woods, which rise several trees from one stump, and, being more tolerant of shade, grow in very dense stand.

It must not be forgotten, however, that a chestnut stump can not go on coppicing forever. With each new generation of sprouts the stump becomes more and more weakened, and hence gradually loses its capacity to produce healthy and vigorous sprouts. Although it is impossible to state with certainty how many generations of chestnut can be raised from the same stock without impairing the vitality of the sprouts, the effects of repeated and bad coppicing manifest themselves in the increasing number of dying chestnuts all over Maryland. The immediate cause of their death can nearly always be traced to attacks of either insects or fungi, yet the prime reason is their decreased vitality, which makes them easy prey for their natural enemies.

The capacity of chestnut to produce sprouts from the stump in spite of the reckless and careless cutting now practiced may delay the entire disappearance of this most desirable of the trees possessed by the farmers of Maryland, but will not save it from deterioration and eventually complete removal, unless efforts are made to provide also for its natural reproduction from the nut. Unless the old trees are replaced from time to time by new ones grown from seed, the woodlot will be gradually thinned of chestnut altogether, for the stumps, especially the old, improperly cut ones, will produce sprouts more and more inferior with each successive generation, until finally they fail entirely to send out shoots.

Although an abundance of seed is borne, the reproduction of chestnut from this source is exceedingly scant in Maryland. This is largely due to the fact that the nuts are a source of revenue. With chestnuts worth on an average $2.50 per bushel delivered in Baltimore (the price often going as low as 60 cents and as high as $5), the gathering of them is usually carried too far for the good of the woodlot. The number of nuts left is insufficient for the natural seedling reproduction of chestnut; and the comparatively few which escape man are greedily devoured by the hogs which range freely in the woods, not to mention the squirrels and crows. If, after all, a chestnut seedling succeeds in coming up, the chances are that it will be destroyed by cattle.

The use of the woodlot as a pasture is one of the chief enemies to the reproduction of the farmers' woods, and chestnut, in this respect, shares only the common fate of all other species. To secure natural reproduction from the nut the woodlot must not be robbed wholly of its crops of chestnuts by turning them into money, the hogs must be kept entirely out of the woods during the season in which chestnuts fall and germinate, or have their presence there restricted to a short time only, and the young chestnut seedlings must be protected from the cattle until they reach the height at which no harm can be done to them. After a young growth of chestnuts from seed is secured it is not necessary to let them mature into large trees; they should be cut in order to provide sprouts, which will reach salable size in a shorter time than the chestnut seedlings could if left to grow undisturbed.

The introduction and application of forest management of any kind must of course be governed by particular conditions in each case, and detailed study is necessary to guide the work. Throughout Maryland the demand for chestnut materials is large and on the increase, and intelligent efforts to supply it are bound to pay eventually. The marketable materials can be supplied more satisfactorily and in a shorter time by coppice than by trees from seed. Post size is reached twice as soon.

TABLE XXII.—*Age at which chestnut is merchantable.*

Kind of product.	Age.	
	Trees from seed.	Coppice.
	Years.	*Years.*
Post	27	14
Tie	41	29
Pole	49	38
Rails	54	43

Timber of large dimensions is furnished principally by chestnut from seed, its slower but more persistent growth enabling it to attain greater height and larger diameter than chestnut coppice. But chestnut is not suited to the production of large timber, on account of its unsoundness and short clear length when it has reached the desired size. Therefore, even if large timber is desirable, chestnut should not stand longer than seventy to eighty years, and coppice will then fill requirements better. Only in exceptional cases, as for the sake of large production of nuts, should chestnut be left standing ninety years or more.

Since reproduction from seed is uncertain under existing conditions, and since the productive capacity of stumps decreases with their age, the cutting of old stands of chestnut should prove of benefit to their owners and the country, provided judgment is used in the logging operations. Many Maryland landowners, especially the old families, have not yet entirely adjusted themselves to the new economic conditions resulting from the civil war. They often let the timber on their woodlots go at a very low price, sometimes as low as 4 cents per tie. The contractors are allowed to cut what, when, and as they please. As a result, the woodlot suffers.

Chestnut should be cut either in winter or early spring. Not only does this assure better reproduction from the stump, but the timber itself will be of better quality and greater durability. When ties are cut in summer and left in the woods for some time, they crack and curl backward at the ends, increasing the number of condemned ties, for which the owner is not paid. Since the owners of woodlots and the contractors are dependent for their labor on the resident colored population, most of whom farm more or less and work in the woods only as a side occupation for additional income, winter is the season when the most reliable laborers can be obtained. Chestnut should be felled with axes, and these should be sharp, so as not to tear the bark loose from the wood. Stumps should be as nearly level with the ground as possible, and the cut surface should slant enough to shed water.

Trees 20 inches or more in diameter breasthigh should be sawed, not hewed, into ties, and no trees smaller than 11 inches should be cut for ties, because the waste in 9-inch and 10-inch trees is out of all proportion to the value of the one tie obtained from them.

O

Printed by Libri Plureos GmbH in Hamburg,
Germany